Snatch Back Your Joy

With the Word of Truth

Wanda M. Brewster

ISBN 979-8-89130-222-8 (paperback)
ISBN 979-8-89130-288-4 (hardcover)
ISBN 979-8-89130-223-5 (digital)

Christian Faith Publishing
832 Park Avenue
Meadville, PA 16335
www.christianfaithpublishing.com

Printed in the United States of America

To my husband, Gregory L. Brewster Sr. (my friend and my king); my daughter, Wendy Brewster-Murphy; my son, Gregory L. Brewster Jr.; and my mother, Ms. Sadie Bell Peters-Davis, who has gone home to be with the Lord.

Contents

Acknowledgments

Special thanks to my husband, Gregory Brewster Sr., and daughter, Wendy Brewster-Murphy, for encouraging me to write this book. All praise and thanksgiving to my Lord and Savior, Jesus Christ, who put the desire in my heart to have the passion for others to snatch their joy back from the enemy! May this book be used to accomplish His will and purpose in the hearts and lives of others who need God's help.

From Rev. Dr. Ellery K. Harris: People will feel the anointing of God as they read this book. This book will open up the pathway of God's Spirit to your Spirit so the Spirit of God may enter and be a guide to your daily living.

Introduction

First and foremost, I want to thank God! He has been with me throughout my life journey even when I didn't know He was watching over me for a time such as this. I am so thankful and grateful that He allowed me to put in a book form from my heart and His Word to share with others. I give God all the HONOR, praise, and glory because, without HIM, I couldn't have shared with you how to change the challenging life situations you may have today!

This book is designed for anyone with some challenging life situations. The book has situations with a quick read for the moment with prayers and powerful scriptures to launch you into a deeper study to help change your life forever! I wanted to reach all who needs something quick and handy in the moment that would point them to God who sent His only begotten Son, Jesus Christ, to die on the cross for our sins and save us from a dying world for eternity.

Forgiveness

This word FORGIVENESS will help, prevent, and hinder a lot of chaos in your life if you STOP quickly and forgive immediately. If left undone, it will wreak havoc in your life and run interference in your relationship with God! Unforgiveness will cause you to lose your identity in life because that is not how God designed you. God is love, and we must walk in the God kind of LOVE.

Scripture References

14 If you forgive those who sin against you, your heavenly Father will forgive you. 15 But if you refuse to forgive others, your Father will not forgive your sins. (Matthew 6:14–15 NLT)

13 Make allowance for each other's faults, and forgive anyone who offends you. Remember, the Lord forgave you, so you must forgive others. 14 Above all, clothe yourselves with love, which binds us all together in perfect harmony. (Colossians 3:13–14)

Prayer

Father, help me to forgive immediately so I can walk in Your love. Help me to remove all bitterness, anger, and any unresolved issues that I have allowed to take root in my heart. Lord, even the unforgiveness that I have not recognized in my heart, please remove and give me a pure heart that I will be fit for Your use and demonstrate Your love to all mankind. Father, I don't want anything to hinder our relationship. Father, make my heart a heart of flesh so I will be quick to forgive. From this day forward, I choose to walk in the light of Your love. In Jesus Name! Amen!

Thoughts and Prayers

Love

If you feel slighted and don't feel LOVE, I want to share with you about the One who created LOVE. His name is GOD—the creator of everything (Genesis 1). In order to LOVE and to be LOVED, we must get to know the Creator of LOVE. Our Father demonstrated LOVE from the very beginning when HE wrapped Himself in a human body through His Son Jesus Christ as a sacrifice to take away our sins. When we truly accept Jesus Christ as our savior and allow God to be the head of our life, LOVE will flow from our hearts because we become who God is without forcing it. We will have a God kind of conscience always walking in genuine love without an excuse.

Scripture References

16 For God loved the world so much that He gave His one and only Son, so that everyone who believes in Him will not perish but have eternal life. (John 3:16)

7 Dear friends, let us continue to love one another, for love comes from God. Anyone who loves is a child of God and knows God. 8 But anyone who does not love does not know God, for God is love. 9 God showed how much He loved us by sending His one and only Son into the world so that we might have eternal life through Him. 10 This is real love—not that

we loved God, but that He loved us and set His Son as a sacrifice to take away our sins. 11 Dear friends, since God loved us that much, we surely ought to love each other. 12 No one has ever seen God. But if we love each other, God lives in us, and His love is brought to full expression in us. 13 And God has given us His Spirit as proof that we live in Him and He in us. 14 Furthermore, we have seen with our own eyes and now testify that the Father sent His Son to be the Savior of the world. 15 All who confess that Jesus is the Son of God have God living in them, and they live in God. 16 We know how much God loves us, and we have put our trust in His love. God is love, and all who live in love live in God, and God lives in them. 17 And as we live in God, our love grows more perfect. So we will not be afraid on the day of judgement, but we can face Him with confidence because we live like Jesus here in this world. 18 Such love has no fear, because perfect love expels all fear. If we are afraid, it is for fear of punishment, and this shows that we have not fully experienced His perfect love. 19 We love each other because He loved us first. 20 If someone says, "I love God," but hates a Christian brother or sister, that person is a liar; for if we don't love people we can see, how can we love God, whom we cannot see? 21 And He has given us this command: Those who love God must also love their Christian brothers and sisters. (1 John 4:7–21)

Prayer

Father, thank You for demonstrating Your love to me and the world by laying down Your life through the person of Your Son, our

Lord and Savior Jesus Christ. Father, help me to walk in Your love. Father, give me the God kind of love for myself and all mankind so that I can effectively communicate with You and allow the demonstration of Your love to flow through me to others. I realize You are LOVE, and the only way to walk in the God kind of love is to allow You to be Lord over my life and communicate with You daily for a lifetime. Father, I surrender my life to You and ask that You live through me so that I can please You here on earth. Let Your light and love shine through me because perfect love expels all fear and darkness. Thank You in advance for allowing me to live like Jesus lived here in this world through the power of love. Jesus made the ultimate sacrifice when He demonstrated His love for us. In Jesus Name! Amen and Amen!

Thoughts and Prayers

Believe

If you are looking for something to believe in and don't know who or what to believe in. In today's society, most people are looking for something or someone to believe in and cling to. I want to introduce you to the One who can help you with your belief. He created you, if you don't know this already. He is God Almighty—the one who not only created you but also created heaven and earth. He has ownership of you, and now, what you need to do is to realize your Owner wants you to believe in Him. God Almighty is the one and only one who can fulfill the void in your heart if you only believe in Him through His only begotten Son Jesus Christ. He will never disappoint you when you put your belief and trust in Him. Since He is the Creator of you, then you must know He can control every situation about you if you allow Him because in the process of His creation, He made you a free will agent. He is only a word away for you to ask Him to take control and help you with your belief. He can then step in and allow new revelations and guidance for your life through the Spirit.

Scripture References

1 In the beginning God created the heavens and the earth. 2 The earth was formless and empty, and darkness covered the deep waters. And the Spirit of God was hovering over the surface of the waters. 3 Then God said, "Let there be light," and there was light. (Genesis 1:1–3 NLT)

27 So God created human beings in His own image. In the image of God He created them; male and female he created them. 28 Then God blessed them and govern it. Reign over the fish in the sea, the birds in the sky, and all the animals that scurry along the ground. (Genesis 1:27–28 NLT)

5 Trust in the LORD with all your hearts, do not depend on your own understanding, 6 Seek His will in all you do, and He will show you which path to take. (Proverbs 3:5–6 NLT)

Prayer

Father God, the creator of the heaven and earth, I ask You today to forgive me for not believing and trusting in You for my life. I ask You to help me with my unbelief and restore a right spirit in me to allow You to lead and guide my life. I thank You for exchanging my carnal mind to a spirit-conscious mind in order for me to move forward and trust You in everything that I do. Father, I will depend on You in all things and put my total trust in the unction of the Holy Spirit to direct my path in Jesus Name! Amen and Amen!

Thoughts and Prayers

Joy

The word *joy* according to *Webster* dictionary is "to experience great pleasure or delight (rejoice). The spiritual definition of joy is "a deep sense of well-being knowing that God has adequate resources to supply all your needs according to His riches in glory through Christ Jesus." There is no need to look for internal joy in things or people because that type of joy will fade away quickly if that is where your joy lies. The God kind of joy will last no matter what is going on around you, and it doesn't depend on what's happening at that moment. The enemy will send surface types of things to steal your joy if you allow him into your dwelling (mind). God will strengthen you when you put your trust in Him and abide in His Word for your life.

Scripture References

10f For the joy of the LORD is your strength. (Nehemiah 8:10f NLT)

7 But if you remain in me and my words remain in you, you may ask for anything you want, and it will be granted! 8 When you produce much fruit, you are My true disciples. This brings great glory to My Father. 9 "I have loved you even as the Father has loved Me. Remain in My love. 10 When you obey My commandments, you remain in My love, just as I obey My

Father's commandments and remain in His love.
11 I have told you these things so that you will
be filled with My joy. Yes, your joy will overflow!"
(John 15:7–11 NLT)

Prayer

Father, thank You for this day You created just for me to rejoice and be glad in You. I come abiding in You as You abide in me that my joy may be filled with Your eternal joy! Thank You for strengthening me so that I can move forward away from the carnal things of this world and rejoice in the things of God. Keeping the enemy (satan) under my feet where he rightfully belongs. I thank You Father for the indwelling of the Holy Spirit in me that He will overflow out of my heart into others so they can experience the God kind of joy for their lives. Thank You for allowing me to produce much fruit that will bring great glory and honor to You! In Jesus Name! Amen and Amen!

Thoughts and Prayers

Grace

Grace is one of those life situations that happens, and we don't have the energy or strength to conquer only what God can work out for us. Grace is God's unmerited favor which we don't deserve. Grace is when God steps in with His divine strength and power to work out a situation we can never do on our own. The word *strength* here is *dunamis*; it means God's wonderful miracle-working power. G-R-A-C-E is God's riches at Christ's expense. When we are up against problems or situations that human strength can't handle is when God's grace can work in your favor if you totally surrender to Him. This is done without your works or resume because God's strength is sufficient and made perfect in ALL HIS WAYS!

Scripture References

9 And he said unto me, My grace is sufficient for thee: for my strength is made perfect in weakness. Most gladly therefore will I rather glory in my infirmities, that the power of Christ may rest upon me. (2 Corinthians 12:9)

8 God saved you by His grace when you believed. And you can't take credit for this; it is a gift from God. 9 Salvation is not a reward for the good things we have done, so none of us can boast about it. 10 For we are God's masterpiece. He has created us anew in Christ Jesus, so we can

do the good things he planned for us long ago.
(Ephesians 2:8–10 NLT)

Prayer

Father, in the Name of Jesus, I thank You for Your unmerited favor that You demonstrated when You sent Your Son, Jesus Christ, to die on the cross for my salvation—a gift that I didn't deserve but You loved me so much that You graced me with the ultimate gift! Father, I rejoice in knowing that Your grace is sufficient in my weakness, and You can heal, deliver, and conquer any problems or situations I face. I am powerless and totally lean on You, Lord. In Jesus Name!

Thoughts and Prayers

Mercy

We should be willing to always extend mercy because this is something God extends to us every morning. God grants us with new mercies every morning when we arise. If we ask trusting and believing God, He has already casted us with new mercies. God never cease to grant us His divine favor and compassion when we ask. He never gives us what we deserve because He is a forgiving and loving God. God always responds with help when we ask for it whether it is what we want or not. God's mercy is greater than any sin or anything that we thought we did or didn't do to deserve His mercy. God doesn't treat us with the punishment that we deserve; instead, He forgives us and gives us hope when we ask. I am not saying you won't face any consequences for your actions; however, you won't receive what you deserve if you ask God and trust Him. God is a faithful, loving God, and He will always honor His promises.

Scripture References

22 The faithful love of the Lord never ends! His mercies never cease. 23 Great is His faithfulness; His mercies begin afresh each morning. (Lamentations 3:22–23 NLT)

6 Praise the Lord! For He has heard my cry for mercy. 7 The Lord is my strength and shield. I trust Him with all my heart. He helps me, and

my heart is filled with joy. I burst out in songs of thanksgiving. (Psalm 28:6–7 NLT)

3 He forgives all my sins and heals all my diseases. 4 He redeems me from death and crowns me with love and tender mercies. (Psalm 103:3–4 NLT)

Prayer

O Merciful Father, thank You for Your mercies that are new every morning, and I am praising You in advance for not giving me what I deserve. Father, I thank You for Your compassion, faithfulness, and the love You demonstrate to me even when I don't deserve it. I thank You for Your faithful love that never ends! I praise Your Holy Name for honoring Your promises and renewing Your mercies toward me afresh and new daily. Father, I will be quick to repent and turn to You when I do anything contrary to Your Word! Father, help me to extend the same mercy and grace to others as You do. I commit to walk in the God kind of mercy toward others. Father, I thank You for the love You poured into my heart through the Holy Spirit given to me as my helper. In Jesus Almighty and Precious Name! Amen and Amen!

Thoughts and Prayers

Faithfulness

God's faithfulness is always in effect toward us. God demonstrated His faithfulness to us from the very beginning when He created us in His image. Since God is always faithful toward us, we need to be faithful and committed to God for His faithfulness to be manifested. God needs us to be faithful to Him so He can use us as a vessel on earth to carry out the ultimate assignments for His will to be done. We as believers need to be faithful so God can trust us with His Word to encourage the unsaved and other believers.

Scripture References

27 So God created human beings in His own image. In the image of God He created them; male and female He created them. 28 Then God blessed them and said, "Be fruitful and multiply. Fill the earth and govern it. Reign over the fish in the sea, the birds in the sky, and all the animals that scurry along the ground." (Genesis 1:27–28 NLT)

8 The Lord is good and does what is right; He shows the proper path to those who go astray. 9 He leads the humble in doing right, teaching them His way. 10 The Lord leads with unfailing love and faithfulness all who keep His covenant and obey His demands. (Psalm 25:8–10 NLT)

Prayer

Father, thank You for creating me in Your image. Help me to obey Your Word and to be faithful toward You. Lord, it is a privilege that I get to share Your Word with others to bring them to a place of decision to commit to You and develop a relationship with You. I thank You for using me as a vessel here on earth to do Your will. Lord, I pray that I will always have a heart of love for Your people. In Jesus Name!

Thoughts and Prayers

Help My Unbelief

Unbelief can be serious and detrimental to your life because if you don't believe in God, you will miss heaven. You are going to believe in something, and that something you believe in other than God will lead you straight to hell, and that is a place for satan and his followers. The only thing that hell has in common with heaven is that they are both free and for eternity! God has sent His only begotten Son, Jesus Christ, to give you hope and an expected end. Unbelief can rob you of your eternal hope and blind you of your future. If you are having trouble believing, just ask God for help; He stands at the door of your heart waiting for you to invite Him in to help you with your unbelief. This is not about a feeling; it is about you believing that God is real through faith and trusting Him with your life for eternity.

Scripture References

57 And they were offended in Him. But Jesus said unto them, A prophet is not without honor, save in His own country, and in His own house. 58 And He did not many mighty works there because of their unbelief. (Matthew 13:57–58)

4 Then Jesus told them, "A prophet is honored everywhere except in His own hometown and among His relatives and His own family."

5 And because of their unbelief, He couldn't do any miracles among them except to place His hands on a few sick people and heal them. 6 And He was amazed at their unbelief. Then Jesus went from village to village, teaching the people. (Mark 6:4–6 NLT)

23 "What do you mean, 'If I can'?" Jesus asked. "Anything is possible if a person believes." 24 The father instantly cried out, "I do believe, but help me overcome my unbelief!" (Mark 9:23–24 NLT)

Prayer

Father, I ask You to forgive me for my unbelief because I have just been going in circles and walking in unbelief trying to do things on my own. I thank You, Lord, that You are giving me another chance to believe and have faith in You. I ask You to come into my heart and strengthen my belief in You so that I will spend eternity with You in heaven. Thank You for giving me a hope and an expected end for the future. Your Word can do the impossible and make thing possible through Jesus Christ! Thank You, Lord! In Jesus Name! Amen!

Thoughts and Prayers

Feelings of Emptiness

The feelings of emptiness can lead you into dangerous territories because you are trying to fill a void in your heart that can only be filled with the love of God. In some cases, it can lead you to choose the wrong friends or do the wrong thing or cause an addiction in your life that can destroy you. When you feel an emptiness in your heart, don't try to fill it with worldly things; seek help from God. If you don't know how to get the help, you need to seek spiritual advice from your pastor or church leaders or counselor or someone you can trust to guide you in the right direction.

Scripture References

7 Casting all your care upon him; for he careth for you. 8 Be sober, be vigilant; because your adversary the devil, as a roaring lion, walketh about, seeking whom he may devour: (1 Peter 5:7–8)

22 Cast thy burden upon the Lord, and he shall sustain thee: He shall never suffer the righteous to be moved. (Psalm 55:22)

1 If ye then be risen with Christ, seek those things which are above, where Christ sitteth on the right hand of God. 2 Set your affection

on things above, not on things on the earth. (Colossians 3:1–2)

17 And if ye call on the Father, who without respect of persons judgeth according to every man's work, pass the time of your sojourning here in fear: 18 forasmuch as ye know that ye were not redeemed with corruptible things, as silver and gold, from your vain conversation received by tradition from your fathers; 19 but with the precious blood of Christ, as of a lamb without blemish and without spot. (1 Peter 1:17–19)

12 For the eyes of the Lord are over the righteous, And his ears are open unto their prayers: But the face of the Lord is against them that do evil. (1 Peter 3:12)

Prayer

Father, I thank You for caring so much about me and being concerned in my feelings of emptiness in my heart. Forgive me for not coming to You sooner and allowing You to fill the void in my heart with Your genuine love. Father, I thank You for allowing me to cast all my burden upon You in exchange for Your love, grace, and mercy. Thank You for destroying the enemy that tried to play tricks in my mind and bring confusion to deter me from trusting You and Your Word for fulfillment. In Jesus Name!

Thoughts and Prayers

Don't Know What I Am Feeling

If you are at a stage in your life and you don't know your purpose or just don't know what you are feeling concerning your life, think about the goodness of God and how He thought you were worst saving; He sent His only begotten Son just for you and me. He sacrificed the Blood of Jesus on the cross so that you can live a productive life for Him here on earth. If you don't know anything else, just know you are loved by God; this is enough to activate your feeling of love. You are worth the Blood of Jesus. There is no one like God on earth or under the earth that can satisfy like He can. Just call on Jesus, Jesus, Jesus when you are in a dark place in your life.

Scripture References

18 For you know that God paid a ransom to save you from the empty life you inherited from your ancestors. And it was not paid with mere gold or silver, which lose their value. 19 It was the precious blood of Christ, the sinless, spotless Lamb of God. 20 God chose Him as your ransom long before the world began, but now in these last days He has been revealed for your sake. 21 Through Christ you have come to trust in God. And you have placed your faith and hope in God because He raised Christ from the dead and gave Him great glory. 22 You were cleansed from your sins when you obeyed the truth, so

now you must show sincere love to each other as brothers and sisters. Love each other deeply with all your heart. (1 Peter 1:18–22 NLT)

Prayer

Father, I thank You for giving Your only begotten Son, Jesus Christ, as a ransom for me. Thank You for allowing me to cast this feeling upon You, and I am going to trust You with the life You have given me to live for You. I realize that it is not about my feeling, but it is all about my relationship with You. Father, thank You for filling my heart with Your love and joy in order for it to flow to others. God, I will, on purpose, spend quality time with You to avoid this stale feeling that had creeped upon me. The joy of the Lord is my strength! In Jesus Name!

Thoughts and Prayers

Peace

The disturbance of your peace can come in many facets or ways to confuse you and to hinder your relationship with God. Christ Himself has brought peace to us through the Blood of Jesus Christ. The devil himself brings anger, bitterness, hostility, division, malice, prejudice (comes in many ways and not just racism), and anything that opposes the things of God. When we walk in unity with our Father God, He gives us peace within our heart to overcome the tactics of the enemy. The Holy Spirit is our helper who will help us through any situation and allows us to look beyond any roadblocks.

Scripture References

12 That at that time you were without Christ, being aliens from the commonwealth of Israel and strangers from the covenants of promise, having no hope and without God in the world. 13 But now in Christ Jesus you who once were far off have been brought near by the blood of Christ. 14 For He Himself is our peace, who has made both one, and has broken down the middle wall of separation, 15 having abolished in His flesh the enmity, *that is,* **the law of commandments** *contained* **in ordinances, so as to create in Himself one new man** *from* **the two,** *thus* **making peace,** 16 and that He might reconcile them both to God in one body through

the cross, thereby putting to death the enmity. 17 And He came and preached peace to you who were afar off and to those who were near. 18 For through Him we both have access by one Spirit to the Father. (Ephesians 2:12–18)

8 Finally, all *of you be* **of one mind, having compassion for one another; love as brothers,** *be* **tenderhearted,** *be* **courteous;** 9 not returning evil for evil or reviling for reviling, but on the contrary blessing, knowing that you were called to this, that you may inherit a blessing. 10 For "He who would love life And see good days, Let him refrain his tongue from evil, And his lips from speaking deceit. 11 Let him turn away from evil and do good; Let him seek peace and pursue it. 12 For the eyes of the LORD *are* **on the righteous,** And His ears *are open* **to their prayers;** But the face of the LORD *is* **against those who do evil.**" (1 Peter 3:8–12)

Prayer

Father, I come to You today thanking You in advance for the Blood of Jesus Christ that gives me hope. I thank You for destroying every tactic the enemy tried to use against me to hinder our relationship. I praise You, Father, for protecting my mind, spirit, and soul from the enemy's plot and plan and rule them to no effect by the Blood of Jesus. Father, from this day forward, I choose to walk in unity with the Lord Jesus Christ. Amen and Amen!

Thoughts and Prayers

Divorce

Divorce is a separation between the union of a man and woman that was joined together through a sacred marriage covenant. However, divorce is not an unpardonable sin because sometimes a divorce is justifiable according to the Word of God when every attempt has been made to avoid separation. (See Matthew 5:31–32 for details.) God is faithful and just to forgive you from all your sins. God sanctioned and ordained all marriages between male and female to last a lifetime. If you are thinking about a divorce, try to ensure you have resolved all measures of the Lord before resulting in a divorce. If you have already divorced and remarried, then don't go on a guilt trip feeling that you are In sin. Remember, God is faithful and just to forgive you from all your sins when you confess, repent, and ask for forgiveness; God restores you back into fellowship with Him.

Scripture References

9 If we confess our sins, He is faithful and just to forgive us our sins and to cleanse us from all unrighteousness. (1 John 1:9)

31 Furthermore it has been said, "Whoever divorces his wife, let him give her a certificate of divorce." 32 But I say to you that whoever divorces his wife for any reason except sexual immorality causes her to commit adultery; and

whoever marries a woman who is divorced commits adultery. (Matthew 5:31–32)

24 Therefore a man shall leave his father and mother and be joined to his wife, and they shall become one flesh. (Genesis 2:24)

4 And He answered and said to them, "Have you not read that He who made them at the beginning 'made them male and female,' 5 and said, 'For this reason a man shall leave his father and mother and be joined to his wife, and the two shall become one flesh'? 6 So then, they are no longer two but one flesh. Therefore what God has joined together, let not man separate." 7 They said to Him, "Why then did Moses command to give a certificate of divorce, and to put her away?" 8 He said to them, "Moses, because of the hardness of your hearts, permitted you to divorce your wives, but from the beginning it was not so. 9 And I say to you, whoever divorces his wife, except for sexual immorality, and marries another, commits adultery; and whoever marries her who is divorced commits adultery." (Matthew 19:4–9)

Prayer

Father, I thank You that You are a forgiving God, and I praise Your Holy Name. Father, only You can restore me back into right fellowship with You through the Blood of Jesus Christ. Father, I repent of all my unfaithful ways (name them) and acts (name them) that are not pleasing in Your sight. Lord, help me to live a righteous life and honor the sacred covenant vow between me and my _________. Lord, I pray that I will never ever return to the ungodly acts (name them) against my _________. Father, I thank You in advance for strengthening me to live a holy life where I will represent You in my lifestyle. God, I praise and worship You with every fiber of my being. Lord, I thank You for Jesus, my mediator, pleading my case with You and the Holy Spirit helping me in my weakness. In Jesus Matchless and Holy Name! Amen and Amen!

Thoughts and Prayers

Stop! You Can't Have My Family

Yes, you have the right command in place to tell satan to STOP and let him know he can't have your family! Command satan to take his hands off your family in the Name of Jesus Christ. Sometimes, you have to stand in the gap for your family members because they may be weak in their flesh. Tell satan the Blood of Jesus is against him, and by Jesus Blood, he has no permission or rights to your family! Whatever sin or addictions that has entrapped your family member/s must be dissolved this day in Jesus Name. Plead the Blood of Jesus in the authority He has given you with the Holy Spirit's help.

Scripture References

17 And the seventy returned again with joy, saying, Lord, even the devils are subject unto us through Thy Name. 18 And He said unto them, I beheld Satan as lightning fall from heaven. 19 Behold, I give unto you power to tread on serpents and scorpions, and over all the power of the enemy: and nothing shall by any means hurt you. (Luke 10:17–19)

26 Then they will come to their senses and escape from the devil's trap. For they have been held captive by him to do whatever he wants. (2 Timothy 2:26 NLT)

10 Who delivered us from so great a death, and doth deliver: in whom we trust that He will yet deliver us; 11 ye also helping together by prayer for us, that for the gift bestowed upon us by the means of many persons thanks may be given by many on our behalf. (2 Corinthians 1:10–11)

19 And for me, that utterance may be given unto me, that I may open my mouth boldly, to make known the mystery of the gospel. (Ephesians 10:19)

Prayer

Father, I thank You that You are a powerful God, and there is none like You in all the earth. You are holy and merciful to us. Father, I thank You that in Your Word, I can open my mouth boldly and command satan to loose __________(family member/s) from his snarl in the Name of Jesus Christ! Thank You that the Blood of Jesus is life and will live on through eternity. God, I trust You that today is deliverance and salvation for __________(family member/s). The Blood of Jesus is against satan and all his antics; they must flee now from ______________ (family member/s) life. Thank You that ________________(family member/s) will live a productive life for You, God. I thank You that every time satan's attacks come against ____________ (family member/s) that they will call upon You, Lord, for their strength and power in their weakness. In Jesus Name!

Thoughts and Prayers

Young Children

Children are a heritage from the Lord, and they are a reward from Him. Children are highly valued in God's kingdom, and we should not take children lightly. God esteems them highly, and we should too; children should not be considered as a burden to you. We all are children at one stage in our life growing into adulthood. Children should be taught, at a young age, about God and His love for them. Teaching and training children at a young age will help them to sustain hardship as they go through life. We should build children up and not belittle them. We should treat children as the gifts they are from the Lord. We should protect young children in every area (molesters, sexual perverts, and deceitful thing) of their life and keep them covered by the Blood of Jesus.

Scripture References

3 Lo, children are a heritage of the LORD: And the fruit of the womb is his reward. (Psalm 127:3)

6 Train up a child in the way he should go: And when he is old, he will not depart from it. (Proverbs 22:6)

15 Foolishness is bound in the heart of a child; But the rod of correction shall drive it far from him. (Proverbs 22:15)

11 Even a child is known by his doings, Whether his work be pure, and whether it be right. (Proverbs 20:11)

4 And, ye fathers, provoke not your children to wrath: but bring them up in the nurture and admonition of the Lord. (Ephesians 6:4)

2 And Jesus called a little child unto him, and set him in the midst of them, 3 and said, Verily I say unto you, Except ye be converted, and become as little children, ye shall not enter into the kingdom of heaven. 4 Whosoever therefore shall humble himself as this little child, the same is greatest in the kingdom of heaven. 5 And whoso shall receive one such little child in my name receiveth me. 6 But whoso shall offend one of these little ones which believe in me, it were better for him that a millstone were hanged about his neck, and that he were drowned in the depth of the sea. (Matthews 18:2–6)

Prayer

Father, thank You for the love You have for young children (or child's name). I ask You to forgive me for any area that I have fallen short in concerning young children (or child's name). Father, help me to teach young children (or child's name) in the way of the Lord and protect them from any hurt, harm, or danger. Father, help me to discern any wrong motive toward young children (or child's name) and expose any attack that try to come up against young children (or child's name). Uncover any plot and plan of the enemy concerning young children (or child's name). In Jesus Name!

Thoughts and Prayers

Adult Children

Adult children still need to be covered in prayer. Although, your child has become an adult by age or left your home, the enemy doesn't stop his attacks; that's why it is important to keep your adult children covered in prayer. This will alleviate worrying if you continue to pray for your adult children. Your prayer will change to a more appropriate prayer for adult children. Your adult child still desires love (sometimes tough), guidance, and direction from their parents. Yes, their ultimate source should always be God, but parenting will continue for a lifetime until the roles are reversed. Our Father in heaven never stops being Father when we accept Him to be Father over our lives.

Scripture References

3 Lo, children are a heritage of the LORD: And the fruit of the womb is his reward. (Psalm 127:3)

19 Arise, cry out in the night: In the beginning of the watches Pour out thine heart like water before the face of the Lord: Lift up thy hands toward him for the life of thy young children, That faint for hunger in the top of every street. (Lamentations 2:19)

28 But if I cast out devils by the Spirit of God, then the kingdom of God is come unto

you. 29 Or else how can one enter into a strong man's house, and spoil his goods, except he first bind the strong man? And then he will spoil his house. 30 He that is not with me is against me; and he that gathereth not with me scattereth abroad. (Matthew 12:28–30)

13 And whatsoever ye shall ask in my name, that will I do, that the Father may be glorified in the Son. 14 If ye shall ask any thing in my name, I will do *it*. (John 14:13–14)

13 Like as a father pitieth his children, So the LORD pitieth them that fear him. 14 For he knoweth our frame; He remembereth that we are dust. 15 As for man, his days are as grass: As a flower of the field, so he flourisheth. (Psalm 103:13–15)

Prayer

Oh gracious Father, I thank You for being the Lord over my life and my family's lives. Thank You for strengthening my adult child(ren) to live a productive and proper life for You here on earth. Father, I plead the Blood of Jesus over my adult child(ren)'s life right now in the Name of Jesus. Thank You for providing all the resource needed to glorify You. I pray that every demonic forces and attack to be destroyed and loosed from _____________ life now in the matchless Name of Jesus Christ. Father, I cancel every assignment sent from the enemy to hinder and block the works of God in _______________life. In the Name of Jesus, I cast every dead works of satan back into the pit from which it came and bind it by the Blood of Jesus Christ for eternity. In Jesus Holy Name!

Thoughts and Prayers

Sickness and Health

God's desire for you is to be healed in your body and in your mind. Healing is freely given by God our Father. He needs us healed so we can fulfill the plan and purpose He has assigned to us here on earth. We must trust God to heal us in our bodies and to make us whole. Jesus gave His life so that we can be healed from sickness and diseases. We must receive our healing by faith, trusting and believing that God will heal us physically or supernaturally as we believe by faith that the Blood of Jesus is enough!

Scripture References

52 And Jesus said unto him, Go thy way; thy faith hath made thee whole. And immediately he received his sight, and followed Jesus in the way. (Mark 10:52)

5 But he *was* **wounded for our transgressions,** *he was* **bruised for our iniquities: the chastisement of our peace** *was* **upon him; and with his stripes we are healed.** (Isaiah 53:5)

2 Bless the Lord, O my soul, And forget not all his benefits: 3 Who forgiveth all thine iniquities; Who healeth all thy diseases; 4 Who redeemeth thy life from destruction; Who

crowneth thee with lovingkindness and tender mercies; (Psalm 103:2–4)

2 Beloved, I wish above all things that thou mayest prosper and be in health, even as thy soul prospereth. (3 John 1:2)

Prayer

Father, I thank You in advance for Your mercies and Your divine healing power. I ask You now if there is anything in my heart that is hindering me from receiving Your divine healing power, please remove it right now in the Name of Jesus. Your Word says Jesus was wounded for my transgressions. He was bruised for my iniquities; the chastisement of my peace is **upon** Him, and with His stripes, I am healed. Thank You, Father, for Your supernatural power and divine intervention to heal and make me whole. Sickness and disease have been ruled null and void in my body now in the Name of Jesus! Thank You, Lord! Thank You, Lord! In the Matchless Name of Jesus Christ!

Thoughts and Prayers

Finances

Finances are something we all need to sustain ourselves while living in this world even though we are not a part of this world; we are just passing through. Walk in faith, trusting and believing God can work miracles in your finances for the resources you need. If you don't have someone providing for you or an income coming in to sustain you, then you must work to obtain finances. Also, trust in God to help you to obtain a job if you are unemployed and need finances to take care of you and your family, if you have a family. Depending on your finances, you may have to work a job that you are not accustomed to doing until a job in your profession is available to bring in resources. The most important thing is to seek God, by faith, trusting and believing for your finances to change.

Scripture References

29 And seek not ye what ye shall eat, or what ye shall drink, neither be ye of doubtful mind. 30 For all these things do the nations of the world seek after: and your Father knoweth that ye have need of these things. 31 But rather seek ye the kingdom of God; and all these things shall be added unto you. (Luke 12:29–31)

5 Trust in the LORD with all thine heart; And lean not unto thine own understanding.

6 In all thy ways acknowledge him, And he shall direct thy paths. (Proverbs 3:5–6)

25 I have been young, and now am old; Yet have I not seen the righteous forsaken, nor His seed begging bread. (Psalm 37:25)

Prayer

Father, I thank You this day that I am surrendering our finances to You and trusting that You are well able to work miracles to sustain me and my family. Thank You for moving by Your power and might to increase our finances. Father, I seek Your face for Your mercies and grace for granting all the resources we need above and beyond we could ever ask or think. Father, Your Word said You know what we have need of, and Your righteous will not be forsaken or begging for bread. Thank You, Father, for providing for us in Jesus Name!

Thoughts and Prayers

Bullying

Bullying in school or anywhere else is a form of evil influences under the power of satan. Usually, the person who is doing the bullying has been hurt and doesn't have the love in their life to feel fulfilled. Also, there are some underlying issues that cause them to take their hurt or frustration out on a timid person with low self-esteem or an insecure person. If you find yourself in either position, this is not of God, and you need to seek help immediately to avoid disaster. If you feel you can't talk to your parents about bullying, always find someone you can talk to or go to the authorities immediately. This doesn't mean you are a failure or fearful; in actuality, this makes you a hero because you put a stop to the plot and plan of the enemy. Don't hesitate when you see bullying, or if you are the one being bullied, always seek help to avoid a catastrophe.

Scripture References

1 Therefore if there is any consolation in Christ, if any comfort of love, if any fellowship of the Spirit, if any affection and mercy, 2 fulfill my joy by being like-minded, having the same love, being of one accord, of one mind. 3 Let nothing be done through selfish ambition or conceit, but in lowliness of mind let each esteem others better than himself. 4 Let each of you look out not only for his own interests, but also for the interests of others. (Philippians 2:1–4)

8 If you really keep the royal law found in Scripture, "Love your neighbor as yourself," you are doing right. (James 2:8 NIV)

7 For God has not given us a spirit of fear, but of power and of love and of a sound mind. (2 Timothy 1:7)

1 The Lord is my light and my salvation; Whom shall I fear? The Lord is the strength of my life; Of whom shall I be afraid? (Psalm 27:1)

Prayer

Father, I thank You for strengthening me in my weakest state to help me to walk in the power of Your love, God. Bullying is not of You, God, and I thank You for being my shield and protector against bullies. Father, You don't give me a spirit of fear but of power, love, and a sound mind that I will trust You when the enemy knocks on my door in the form of bullying. God, I ask You to fill _______________ with the love of God or illuminate the issues/problems in _______________ life that are causing them to act in such a manner of bullying. Lord, I thank You for putting the right person in my life to resolve this issue quickly. Father, I thank You that vengeance is Yours, and I release all my troubles into Your hand. In Jesus Name!

Thoughts and Prayers

You Feel There Is Nowhere to Turn

When you feel there is nowhere to turn, there is always somewhere to turn or somebody to turn to if your heart is willing to surrender to the Great and Mighty One (GOD). You can never exhaust all your options with God because He said in His Word that He will never leave you nor forsake you. God is always a knock or a listening ear away, and He will lead you in the right direction through the unction of the Holy Spirit. If you don't know who God is, then seek counsel from your pastor, a church leader or a spiritual adviser to help you; one of them should be able to introduce you to God the Father, Jesus Christ, the Son, and the Holy Spirit. This will get you started with the hope, joy, and comfort you need to move forward and away from the enemy's trick. Even if you need to seek some professional help, God has the right assistant in place to help you, so don't be dismayed or fall for the enemy's tricks and devices.

Scripture References

8 And the LORD, He is the One who goes before you. He will be with you, He will not leave you nor forsake you; do not fear nor be dismayed. (Deuteronomy 31:8)

5 Let your conduct be without covetousness; be content with such things as you have. For He Himself has said, "I will never leave you nor forsake you." (Hebrews 13:5)

8 But what does it say? "The word is near you, in your mouth and in your heart" (that is, the word of faith which we preach): 9 that if you confess with your mouth the Lord Jesus and believe in your heart that God has raised Him from the dead, you will be saved. 10 For with the heart one believes unto righteousness, and with the mouth confession is made unto salvation. 11 For the Scripture says, "Whoever believes on Him will not be put to shame." (Romans 10:8–11)

13 For "whoever calls on the name of the Lord shall be saved." (Romans 10:13)

[Ephesians 1:3; 1 Peter 1:3] 3 Blessed be the God and Father of our Lord Jesus Christ, the Father of mercies and God of all comfort, 4 who comforts us in all our tribulation, that we may be able to comfort those who are in any trouble, with the comfort with which we ourselves are comforted by God. 5 For as the sufferings of Christ abound in us, so our consolation also abounds through Christ. (2 Corinthian 1:3–5)

Prayer

Father, thank You for being my help and comfort in such trying times when I felt there was nowhere else to turn. O God, I thank You for giving me comfort and hope to know that You will never leave me comfortless. Thank You for strengthening me against the enemy that tries to invade my heart and mind with lies. Father, I praise You for never leaving me or forsaking me! I can move forward in You knowing that You are with me. Thank You for the people You have put in my path to encourage me in Your Word and the ones who assisted me in seeking the help I needed to realize there is hope in You! Father, I have the assurance now that I can always turn to You for guidance in troublesome time. In Jesus Name!

Thoughts and Prayers

Stop, You Can't Have My Children

Your children are an inheritance from God; the fruit of the womb is a reward. When satan and his antics try to take your children from you and introduce them to the ways of the world, keep your focus on God no matter what it looks like in the natural. Plead the Blood of Jesus over your children, and don't give up on them because God didn't give up on you. The enemy will create all kinds of trouble and will wreak havoc with your children; if you don't keep them covered by the Blood of Jesus, he will try to destroy them. Always teach your children the Word of God so they will have some substance to hold on to when the enemy comes after them. Know that God is still in control when you pray believing HIM at His Word.

Scripture References

3 Behold, children are a heritage from the LORD, The fruit of the womb is a reward. (Psalm 127:3)

10 The thief does not come except to steal, and to kill, and to destroy. I have come that they may have life, and that they may have it more abundantly. (John 10:10)

19 Behold, I give you the authority to trample on serpents and scorpions, and over all the

power of the enemy, and nothing shall by any means hurt you. (Luke 10:19)

Prayer

Father God, I come to You in the Name of Jesus Christ thanking You for entrusting me with Your heritage, Your precious child(ren). Your Word says children are a heritage from You, and the fruit of the womb is a reward. Lord, I pray that this day, satan has to take his hands off what You have deemed to be Your heritage. I plead the Blood of Jesus over my child(ren), and by the authority You have given me through Jesus Christ, the enemy has to flee from my child(ren)'s life and can no longer dominate their life. God, I thank You that my child(ren) will live in abundance. Father, I thank You for bringing back to remembrance to my child(ren) the Word of God when the enemy tries to steal, kill, and destroy their life. In Jesus Name!

Thoughts and Prayers

Addiction

Addictions are from satan's assonant to keep you from being developed in your full potential of life that God has purposed for you to live. God has sent His only begotten Son, Jesus Christ, so that you can live a life dedicated to HIM for His glory! Only the power of God through prayer can break the stronghold of addictions the enemy has inflicted upon you. An addiction can be any habit that contradict the Word of God and has such a stronghold on you that you can't resist the urgency of doing it. Don't be too proud or ashamed to seek help if you need a prayer partner or battle buddy to help you be delivered from an addiction. Remember, God is enough because He created you from the very beginning; after the fall of man, He sent His only begotten Son, Jesus Christ, to rescue you. Jesus Christ sent a helper after you accepted Him as your personal savior. Believe in God and yourself!

Scripture References

16 As for me, I will call upon God; And the LORD **shall save me.** 17 Evening, and morning, and at noon, will I pray, and cry aloud: And He shall hear my voice. 18 He hath delivered my soul in peace from the battle *that was* **against me: For there were many with me.** (Psalm 55:16–18)

32 And ye shall know the truth, and the truth shall make you free. 36 If the Son therefore

shall make you free, ye shall be free indeed. (John 8: 32, 36)

20 He sent his word, and healed them, and delivered them from their destructions. (Psalm 107:20)

19 Many *are* **the afflictions of the righteous:** But the LORD **delivereth him out of them all.** (Psalm 34:19)

Prayer

Father, I pray in the Name of Jesus that You will forgive me of this terrible affliction that has come upon me. I ask for Your strength to stand against the enemy's attacks and Your power to resist this addiction/s of _____________________ that I have indulged in for too long. Thank You for delivering me from the plans of destruction of satan that tried to destroy me. Thank You for healing my mind and delivering me from any strongholds in my life. I abide in You and Your Word for strength to overcome. Lord, I will put my trust in You and depend totally in Your Word from this day forward. Lord, thank You for quenching my craving for unhealthy things and allowing me to thirst after You. Thank You for giving me the discernment to know when things are sent to destroy me in the Name of Jesus. Father, I am free and will remain free! In Jesus Holy Name!

Thoughts and Prayers

Liar

The father of a liar is the devil himself. A liar is a person who speak untruth and is operating under the influence of the enemy. God is the truth, and He has sent Jesus to set us free from the snare of satan, the father of lies. If you are having trouble discerning the truth, seek God, and the Holy Spirit will lead you into all truth. Satan comes with a bag of lies and tricks to distract you from the real truth (Jesus), and then he will deceive you to expose the things that are not of God. Stay focused on the Word of God to discern the truth to remain free from the enemy.

Scripture References

44 You are of *your* **father the devil, and the desires of your father you want to do.** He was a murderer from the beginning, and does not stand in the truth, because there is no truth in him. When he speaks a lie, he speaks from his own *resources,* **for he is a liar and the father of it.** 45 But because I tell the truth, you do not believe Me. 46 Which of you convicts Me of sin? And if I tell the truth, why do you not believe Me? 47 He who is of God hears God's words; therefore you do not hear, because you are not of God. (John 8:44–47)

5 Every word of God *is* **pure; He** *is* **a shield to those who put their trust in Him.** 6 Do not add to His words, Lest He rebuke you, and you be found a liar. (Proverbs 30:5–6)

2 In hope of eternal life, which God, that cannot lie, promised before the world began. (Titus 1:2)

Prayer

Father, thank You for being the Father of all truth. I pray that You would help me with my discernment of all lies from the enemy. Thank You, Father, for exposing every trick the enemy tries to exert in my life. I will believe the truth from God because God will not lie and cannot lie. Thank You for the Blood of Jesus that came to free me from the snare of the enemy's lies. I choose to walk in truth and the Word of God so I can be shielded from the devil's lies. I will not receive a life from the devil and I will speak the truth at all times before my Father. I rebuke every lying spirit that tries to attach itself to me in Jesus Name!

Thoughts and Prayers

Worrying

Worrying is one of satan's devices that can cause sickness in your body. Instead of worrying, you need to cast whatever situation or circumstance upon the Lord for He is the Master of solving problems. You should ask God to help you with things that are greater than you or beyond your control. Yes, we have some challenging things that will come our way, but one thing is for sure: God is able to move mountains and turn things around in His timing. When you trust God, He is able to change the impossible to possible.

Scripture References

6 Be careful for nothing; but in everything by prayer and supplication with thanksgiving let your requests be made known unto God. 7 And the peace of God, which passeth all understanding, shall keep your hearts and minds through Christ Jesus. (Philippians 4:6–7)

7 Casting all your care upon him; for He careth for you. 8 Be sober, be vigilant; because your adversary the devil, as a roaring lion, walketh about, seeking whom he may devour: 9 whom resist steadfast in the faith, knowing that the same afflictions are accomplished in your brethren that are in the world. (1 Peter 5:7–9)

23 For verily I say unto you, That whosoever shall say unto this mountain, Be thou removed, and be thou cast into the sea; and shall not doubt in his heart, but shall believe that those things which He saith shall come to pass; He shall have whatsoever he saith. 24 Therefore I say unto you, What things soever ye desire, when ye pray, believe that ye receive *them*, and ye shall have *them*. (Mark 11:23–24)

Prayer

Father, thank You for caring for me enough to resolve this situation that is greater than I. I thank You for moving mountains that You didn't intend for me to carry in my life. I am casting all my cares and burdens upon You because I am trusting You at Your Word without any doubt in my heart. Thank You for being the Master of my life and removing _________ from my life today, in Jesus Name. I thank You for strengthening me as I trust You by faith in Jesus Holy Name!

Thoughts and Prayers

Happiness

Happiness is a state of feeling when you are in the moment that can fade away depending on what's going on around you. Happiness is more of a surface type of joy instead of an internal feeling that you get when you have internal joy. You want to ensure you don't misconstrue happiness with joy. Happiness is in the moment of activities or festivities, and when the activities or festivities ends, your happiness is gone. You want to seek after internal joy that will last no matter what is going on around you. True happiness will come, and the Holy Spirit will develop it in you as you read the Word of God and cultivate your relationship with God. It is okay to be happy, but ensure you balance it with JOY—*a deep sense of well-being knowing that God has enough adequate resources to keep your internal joy no matter what is going on around you or in you.*

Scripture References

6 My days fly faster than a weaver's shuttle. They end without hope. 7 O God, remember that my life is but a breath, and I will never again feel happiness. (Job 7:6–7 NLT)

25 My life passes more swiftly than a runner. It flees away without a glimpse of happiness. (Job 9:25 NLT)

34 Give me understanding and I will obey your instructions; I will put them into practice with all my heart. 35 Make me walk along the path of your commands, for that is where my happiness is found. (Psalm 119:34–35 NLT)

3 Be merciful to me, O Lord, for I am calling on you constantly. 4 Give me happiness, O Lord, for I give myself to you. 5 O Lord, you are so good, so ready to forgive, so full of unfailing love for all who ask for your help. (Psalm 86:3–5 NLT)

Prayer

O Lord, I ask You to forgive me for depending on surface types of things to make me happy instead of depending on You and Your Word. Father, I ask You to fill me with Your internal joy that will sustain my happiness no matter what is going on around me. Thank You, Lord, that my hope and joy is in You and not the happenstance that is going on at the moment. Amen and Amen!

Thoughts and Prayers

Weakness

If you feel you have succumbed to a point of just weakness in your body, spirit, and soul, then God has enough strength to strengthen you in your weakness. He is just a request away waiting for you to depend on Him to sustain you in your weakest moment. God has always had us on His mind when He sent His only begotten Son, Jesus Christ, to rescue us from a dying world. God has granted us with mercies and grace in heavenly places. Jesus came and rescued us, then He sent us the Helper, the Holy Spirit, to help us in our weakest infirmities. When you feel you are weak and at your lowest state, always remember God will stand up for you through His greatest sacrifice in Jesus Christ!

Scripture References

23 Who remembered us in our low estate: For his mercy endureth for ever: 24 And hath redeemed us from our enemies: For his mercy endureth for ever. 25 Who giveth food to all flesh: For his mercy endureth for ever. (Psalm 136:23–25)

3 For what the law could not do, in that it was weak through the flesh, God sending his own Son in the likeness of sinful flesh, and for sin, condemned sin in the flesh: 4 that the righteousness of the law might be fulfilled in us, who walk

not after the flesh, but after the Spirit. 5 For they that are after the flesh do mind the things of the flesh; but they that are after the Spirit the things of the Spirit. (Romans 8:3–5)

Prayer

Father, I thank You for giving me the strength to go on because I am at my weakest point right now, and I need Your help in this situation __________ or what I am feeling that has come upon me. God Almighty, I thank You for sending Your Son, Jesus Christ, to carry this burden/s__________ that I am not able to carry. Thank You, God, for Your mercy and grace that are able to strengthen me to move forward this day in Jesus Name. I receive Your divine strength and power that has broken the stronghold off my life now. Thank You, Jesus, for being the ultimate sacrifice for me. Glory Hallelujah!

Thoughts and Prayers

No Situation Is Too Great for Our God

There is no situation too great for our God. God formed the universe and everything in it. Therefore, nothing can conquer the Owner because He knows the ins and outs of His creation. If you are seeking help or looking for answers, seek the one who created you. God has given instructions and guidance in the Bible for everything under the sun that you may encounter on earth. Search the Word of God for answers!

Scripture References

1 In the beginning God created the heavens and the earth. 2 The earth was without form, and void; and darkness was on the face of the deep. And the Spirit of God was hovering over the face of the waters. 3 Then God said, "Let there be light"; and there was light. 4 And God saw the light, that it was good; and God divided the light from the darkness. 5 God called the light Day, and the darkness He called Night. So the evening and the morning were the first day. (Genesis 1:1–5)

Prayer

Father, thank You for creating me and leaving me instructions for the situations and circumstances that I have encountered. Lord, thank You for leading me to the right guidance and instructions for my life. Thank You, Lord, for empowering me with Your Word that I will follow the Holy Spirit's guidance that has been given to me as a helper. Father, I will seek Your Word for the directions I need to follow. In Jesus Name!

Thoughts and Prayers

Job

If you are in pursuit of a job and seeking guidance or direction for employment. First, you must seek God through Jesus Christ for guidance and direction in pursuit of your heart's desire for your career or employment. God knows the end from the beginning; seek Him, and He will give you peace in the midst of your struggles in searching for a job. Trust and have faith in God as you search for a job. He will provide you with a job because He is obligated to provide for His children. If He will provide for the birds of the air, surely, He will provide for His children that He sent His only begotten Son to die for.

Scripture References

26 Look at the birds of the air, for they neither sow nor reap nor gather into barns; yet your heavenly Father feeds them. Are you not of more value than they? 27 Which of you by worrying can add one cubit to his stature? (Matthew 6:26–27)

31 Therefore do not worry, saying, "What shall we eat?" or "What shall we drink?" or "What shall we wear?" 32 For after all these things the Gentiles seek. For your heavenly Father knows that you need all these things. 33 But seek first the kingdom of God and His righteousness, and all

these things shall be added to you. 34 Therefore do not worry about tomorrow, for tomorrow will worry about its own things. Sufficient for the day is its own trouble. (Matthew 6:31–34)

16 For God so loved the world that He gave His only begotten Son, that whoever believes in Him should not perish but have everlasting life. (John 3:16)

Prayer

Father, thank You for Your divine insight and revelation for my life as I search for a job to provide for my well-being. I want to thank You in advance for providing the job in my career field to enhance my skills and abilities to please You. Father, my desire is to be a witness for You in whatever job You assigned me to. Lord, I realize that I am not my own and that You redeemed me back to You as Your very own when You sent Your Son Jesus Christ to die on the cross for my sins. In Jesus Holy Name!

Thoughts and Prayers

Confusion

The author of confusion is satan; he brings chaos into your life as a distraction to try to void out the peace that God has bestowed upon you. Confusion distorts your mind so you will not be able to function properly and cause you not to make wise decisions. Confusion is like a jungle that is running rapid in your mind when it is untamed. God wants your mind whole so you can make decisive and effective decisions. As you read the Word of God and praise Him, this will block satan's antics from clouding your mind with poor judgments. God has given you the mind of Christ, the heart of God and filled you with the Holy Spirit to alleviate the chaos from your life.

Scripture References

33 For God is not the author of confusion, but of peace. (1 Corinthians 14:33)

7 For God hath not given us the spirit of fear; but of power, and of love, and of a sound mind. (2 Timothy 1:7)

16 For who hath known the mind of the Lord, that he may instruct him? But we have the mind of Christ. (1 Corinthians 2:16)

16 For where envying and strife is, there is confusion and every evil work. 17 But the

wisdom that is from above is first pure, then peaceable, gentle, and easy to be intreated, full of mercy and good fruits, without partiality, and without hypocrisy. 18 And the fruit of righteousness is sown in peace of them that make peace. (James 3:16–18)

6 Be careful for nothing; but in everything by prayer and supplication with thanksgiving let your requests be made known unto God. 7 And the peace of God, which passeth all understanding, shall keep your hearts and minds through Christ Jesus. (Philippians 4:6–7)

Prayer

Father, I thank You for Your divine protection over my mind so that I can make sound decisions and judgments. Thank You, God, for allowing me to avoid confusion and live in peace with all men. Thank You for strengthening me to discern any tactics and antics the devil bring my way or try to invoke in my life. Lord, thank You for not giving me a spirit of fear but power, love, and a sound mind. O God, thank You for the peace of God which passeth all my understanding that will keep my heart and mind through Christ Jesus. Amen and Amen!

Thoughts and Prayers

Trust

First and foremost, we should put our trust in God and allow Him to lead us in this area of trusting. When we put our trust in God through prayer and believing in Him, then we can expect a favorable expectation as the result. You must trust God completely because your mind can play tricks on you when you allow self to get involved. You know where the bag of tricks come from, and it is not God's (the enemy himself brings counterfeits). God will give you wisdom and make you wise beyond your own intellect when you totally trust Him. God leads, guides, and direct your path to perfection when He is the leader.

Scripture References

5 Trust in the LORD with all thine heart; And lean not unto thine own understanding. 6 In all thy ways acknowledge him, And He shall direct thy paths. 7 Be not wise in thine own eyes: Fear the LORD, and depart from evil. (Proverbs 3:5–7)

31 As for God, his way is perfect; The word of the LORD is tried: He is a buckler to all them that trust in Him. 32 For who is God, save the LORD? And who is a rock, save our God? 33 God is my strength and power: And He maketh my way perfect. (2 Samuel 22:31–33)

7 Some trust in chariots, and some in horses: But we will remember the name of the LORD our God. 8 They are brought down and fallen: But we are risen, and stand upright. (Psalm 20:7–8)

3 Trust in the LORD, and do good; So shalt thou dwell in the land, and verily thou shalt be fed. 4 Delight thyself also in the LORD; And He shall give thee the desires of thine heart. 5 Commit thy way unto the LORD; Trust also in him; And he shall bring it to pass. (Psalm 37:3–5)

41 Let thy mercies come also unto me, O LORD, Even thy salvation, according to thy word. 42 So shall I have wherewith to answer him that reproacheth me: For I trust in Thy Word. (Psalm 119:41–42)

4 But as we were allowed of God to be put in trust with the gospel, even so we speak; not as pleasing men, but God, which trieth our hearts. (1 Thessalonians 2:4)

Prayer

Father, I ask You to forgive me in the area of trust; I have fallen short in this area, but I know what Your Word says about me leaning not unto my own understanding and that I should acknowledge You in all my ways. Lord, I ask You for strength to overcome this fear of trusting and completely put my trust in You. Lord, today, I am putting my trust in You and believing that by Your power and might, this situation/s _______________ will come to pass in Your perfection in Jesus Name!

Thoughts and Prayers

Occult

Occult (otherworldly, confused, criminal, ungodly, and traitors) is from satan and used to manipulate and deceive people. Occult is otherworldly agencies that operates outside of godly principles and beliefs. The truth is not in them! Occult is an agency that invokes evil powers and rebels against God and His authority. This agency is partnered with satan and his followers. If you are invited to participate or join an organization that opposes godly principles, then this is an occult that you should not be a part of; immediately remove yourself. Also, seek help if you find yourself in danger and need assistance in separating yourself from any agency. There are many agencies that operate under the influence of an occult, to name a few: gangs, witches, sorcery, divination, mediums and psychic, black magic. There are otherworldly agencies not listed; remember, anything that opposes God and His authority is an occult. Seek more research for additional knowledge.

Scripture References

18 You shall not permit a sorceress to live. Exodus 22:18

6 Also he made his son pass through the fire, practiced soothsaying, used witchcraft, and consulted spiritists and mediums. He did much evil in the sight of the Lord, to provoke Him to anger. (2 King 21:6)

10 There shall not be found among you anyone who makes his son or his daughter pass through the fire, or one who practices witchcraft, or a soothsayer, or one who interprets omens, or a sorcerer, 11 or one who conjures spells, or a medium, or a spiritist, or one who calls up the dead. 12 For all who do these things are an abomination to the Lord, and because of these abominations the Lord your God drives them out from before you. 13 You shall be blameless before the Lord your God. (Deuteronomy 18:10–13)

18 And many who had believed came confessing and telling their deeds. 19 Also, many of those who had practiced magic brought their books together and burned them in the sight of all. And they counted up the value of them, and it totaled fifty thousand pieces of silver. 20 So the word of the Lord grew mightily and prevailed. (Acts 19:18–20)

Prayer

Father, I come to You as humble as I can asking You to forgive me for seeking other gods and principles that goes against You. Lord, I thank You for allowing me to see the attacks of satan and his followers. Lord, thank You for revealing to me the lies, schemes, and tricks of the devil. Thank You for loving me enough to remove me from the snare of the enemy and all the deception that satan tried to deceive me with. God, I give myself to You for You to create in me a clean heart so I can be a vessel You can use in the kingdom to bring glory and honor to You! I am so grateful You didn't leave me in the hands of the enemy. Lord, I praise Your righteous and Holy Name! In Jesus Name!

Thoughts and Prayers

Wisdom

If you are seeking wisdom, your first and foremost seeking should be from God. God instructs us in His Word that if we lack wisdom, we must ask Him for it. Wisdom is not based on your intellect or how smart you are in the flesh. The wisdom that God gives will make you wise above your natural knowledge and understanding. God's divine wisdom allows you do things or make decisions you would have never thought of until God activated His power within you. So whatever you are facing today and you need God's wisdom, ask in prayer following the leading and guiding of the Holy Spirit.

Scripture References

5 If any of you lack wisdom, let him ask of God, that giveth to all men liberally, and upbraideth not; and it shall be given him. 6 But let him ask in faith, nothing wavering. For he that wavereth is like a wave of the sea driven with the wind and tossed. (James 1:5–6)

6 For the LORD giveth wisdom: Out of his mouth cometh knowledge and understanding. 7 He layeth up sound wisdom for the righteous: He is a buckler to them that walk uprightly. (Proverbs 2:6–7)

2 That their hearts might be comforted, being knit together in love, and unto all riches of the full assurance of understanding, to the acknowledgement of the mystery of God, and of the Father, and of Christ; 3 in whom are hid all the treasures of wisdom and knowledge. (Colossians 2:2–3)

Prayer

Father, I am lacking in Your wisdom and knowledge doing this challenging time. Thank You for Your wisdom and knowledge that money can't buy. Your Word says if I lack wisdom, I can ask of You. I am thanking You in advance for Your divine intervention in this situation/s (________________). Father, teach me Your way by the unction of the Holy Spirit that will lead and guide me into all perfection according to Your Word. God, I know that true wisdom only comes from You. Thank You, Lord, in Jesus Holy Name! Amen and Amen!

Thoughts and Prayers

Sin

Sin is anything that God is not pleased with according to the Word of God. That is why it is so important to read and study the Word of God for wisdom and knowledge to build your relationship with God. Knowing God will help you to determine if you have committed a sin or not according to His Word. There is no big sin or little sin; sin is sin. You have an enemy that is always at your door influencing you to sin against God. You may be wondering, *Well, is there anyone who doesn't commit sin?* Well, we all sin in one fashion or another. The main thing is that you don't stay in your sin, and you don't habitually sin—keep sinning over and over again. The Word of God says we all have sinned and come short. (Romans 3:23 says for all have sinned and come short of the glory of God.) We must be quick to repent to keep the Blood of Jesus Christ covering in and over our life.

Scripture References

10 As it is written, There is none righteous, no, not one: (John 3:10)

21 And she shall bring forth a son, and thou shalt call his name Jesus: for he shall save his people from their sins. (Matthews 1:21)

29 The next day John seeth Jesus coming unto him, and saith, Behold the Lamb of God, which taketh away the sin of the world. (John 1:29)

38 Then Peter said unto them, Repent, and be baptized every one of you in the name of Jesus Christ for the remission of sins, and ye shall receive the gift of the Holy Ghost. (Acts 2:38)

9 If we confess our sins, he is faithful and just to forgive us our sins, and to cleanse us from all unrighteousness. 10 If we say that we have not sinned, we make him a liar, and his word is not in us. (1 John 1:9–10)

3 Grace be to you and peace from God the Father, and from our Lord Jesus Christ, 4 who gave himself for our sins, that he might deliver us from this present evil world, according to the will of God and our Father: 5 to whom be glory for ever and ever. Amen. (Galatians 1:3–5)

10 The thief cometh not, but for to steal, and to kill, and to destroy: I am come that they might have life, and that they might have it more abundantly. (John 10:10)

Prayer

Father, thank You for forgiving me of my sins, big or little. I realize that I have sinned against You, and I repent of my sin/s______________ this day in Jesus Name. Thank You, Father, for sending Jesus to save me from this dying world so that I can be free from sin and the attacks of the enemy that comes to steal, kill, and destroy my life. Father, I am so grateful and thankful for You providing a way for me not to stay in sin. I confess today that I will not turn back to the ways of the world that is designed to destroy me in Jesus Name! Amen and Amen!

Thoughts and Prayers

Praise

Praise is what we get to do unto our Almighty God because we love Him and He loved us first. Praise looks good on you, and God is pleased with you when you offer Him a sacrifice of praise. God desires all the praise and honor; he created the universe and all mankind. You may wonder why you can't praise the Almighty God when you see others around you dancing, singing, and jumping for joy. They have experienced the goodness of the Lord, and they know what God has done for them. It is not necessary that it is material or tangible things, but it could be as simple as PEACE AND JOY in their lives. You see, if you are downcast and dead inside, you can't praise God. The enemy has your faculties on lock; don't give him any control over your life. You got to come alive on the inside to praise God's Holy Name! Don't allow the enemy to feed you the trick that you can praise God by not opening your mouth or lifting your hands (this is not for someone with a disability, and they can't lift their hands or speak). God said praise is commonly for the upright. Imagine all on one accord in the sanctuary and God seated in the midst because unity is where He commands the blessing.

Scripture References

1 Rejoice in the LORD, O ye righteous: For praise is comely for the upright. 2 Praise the LORD with harp: Sing unto Him with the psaltery and an instrument of ten strings. (Psalm 33:1–2)

23 Whoso offereth praise glorifieth Me: And to him that ordereth his conversation aright will I shew the salvation of God. (Psalm 50:23)

1 Praise ye the LORD. Sing unto the LORD a new song, And his praise in the congregation of saints. (Psalm 149:1)

1 O LORD, thou art my God; I will exalt thee, I will praise thy name; for thou hast done wonderful things; thy counsels of old are faithfulness and truth. (Isaiah 25:1)

18 For the grave cannot praise thee, death cannot celebrate thee: They that go down into the pit cannot hope for Thy Truth. 19 The living, the living, he shall praise thee, as I do this day: The Father to the children shall make known Thy Truth. 20 The LORD was ready to save me: Therefore we will sing my songs to the stringed instruments All the days of our life in the house of the LORD. (Isaiah 38:18–20)

21 This people have I formed for myself; they shall shew forth My praise. (Isaiah 43:21)

15 By Him therefore let us offer the sacrifice of praise to God continually, that is, the fruit of *our* **lips giving thanks to** His Name. 16 But to do good and to communicate forget not: for with such sacrifices God is well pleased. (Hebrew 13:15–16)

9 But ye are a chosen generation, a royal priesthood, a holy nation, a peculiar people; that ye should shew forth the praises of Him who

hath called you out of darkness into His marvelous light: (1 Peter 2:9)

Prayer

Father, I praise Your Holy Name, and I ask You to forgive me where I have fallen short in giving You all the praise and honor that is due Your name. I will no longer allow any dead unprofitable things to hinder praising You. God, You are worthy of all the praise, and I reverence You! You, the Great Shepherd and Almighty God. I will sing; I will dance, and I will lift hands giving You all the praise all the days of my life. In Jesus Name!

Thoughts and Prayers

Worship

Worship is a lifestyle of reverence unto the Lord! In whatever you do, God should get the glory, and it should magnify His Holy Name. Some people think it is a posture or a song that you offer unto God. Well, that is not all; we should worship God through prayer, praise, our conduct, through our conversation, attitude, songs, and with a reverential fear of the Lord (this is not a spooky type of fear). God wants us to worship Him in spirit and in truth sending a sweet-smelling aroma into His nostrils. God deserves all the glory and honor that is due His Holy Name. Imagine all worshipping God with all hearts on one accord in the sanctuary and God seated in the midst because unity is where He commands the blessing. This would be an awesome visitation from God.

Scripture References

16 Let the word of Christ dwell in you richly in all wisdom, teaching and admonishing one another in psalms and hymns and spiritual songs, singing with grace in your hearts to the Lord. 17 And whatever you do in word or deed, do all in the name of the Lord Jesus, giving thanks to God the Father through Him. (Colossians 3:16–17)

23 But the hour is coming, and now is, when the true worshipers will worship the Father

in spirit and truth; for the Father is seeking such
to worship Him. 24 God is Spirit, and those who
worship Him must worship in spirit and truth.
(John 4:23–24)

22 Since you have purified your souls in
obeying the truth through the Spirit in sincere
love of the brethren, love one another fervently
with a pure heart. (1 Peter 1:22)

13 In Him you also trusted, after you heard
the word of truth, the gospel of your salvation; in
whom also, having believed, you were sealed with
the Holy Spirit of promise. (Ephesians 1:13)

17 The Spirit of truth, whom the world
cannot receive, because it neither sees Him nor
knows Him; but you know Him, for He dwells
with you and will be in you. (John 14:17)

Prayer

Father, I praise Your righteous and Holy Name! I thank You
that I get to worship You in Spirit and in truth. It is a privilege to
worship You because of Your unfailing love that You demonstrate
to me each and every day that I wake up. Father, I give You glory.
Hallelujah! Father, help me and teach me Your way, O God, that
I will serve You in Spirit and in truth. I want to please You, Lord.
Lord, thank You for illuminating the Holy Spirit in me with Your
Word that whatever I do in word or deed will bring honor and glory
to You. Father, I thank You for allowing Your love to flow through
me to others so that they can feel and sense Your presence near them.
Father, thank You for abiding in me as Your dwelling place through
the power of the Holy Spirit. Father, I sing unto You a new song in
the attitude of worship and adoration. I worship You in Spirit and
truth with my life in Jesus Name!

Thoughts and Prayers

Pride

Pride is when you exalt yourself above others with an ego of self-gratification. Pride is the opposite of humility. If you are not careful, you can easily allow yourself to walk in deceit and in vainglory. Don't allow pride to be misplaced with confidence; it is okay to be confident if you don't allow your confidence to be replaced with arrogance or conceitedness or egotism (to name a few). You should have faith in yourself and be confident that you will achieve the plans and goals that God has for your life. God gives grace to the humble as you submit yourself to the Word of God. Allow the Word of God to take root in your heart to avoid destruction from the satan.

Scripture References

13 The fear of the Lord is to hate evil; Pride and arrogance and the evil way and the perverse mouth I hate. (Proverbs 8:13)

2 When pride comes, then comes shame; But with the humble is wisdom. (Proverbs 11:2)

10 By pride comes nothing but strife, but with the well-advised is wisdom. (Proverbs 13:10)

3 In the mouth of a fool is a rod of pride, but the lips of the wise will preserve them. (Proverbs 14:3)

18 Pride goes before destruction, and a haughty spirit before a fall. (Proverbs 16:18)

24 A proud and haughty man—"Scoffer" is his name; He acts with arrogant pride. (Proverbs 21:24)

23 A man's pride will bring him low, But the humble in spirit will retain honor. (Proverbs 29:23)

Prayer

Father, thank You for Your wisdom and guidance on how to avoid walking in a prideful way. I thank You for giving me this opportunity to walk in a spirit of humility as Your Word has instructed me to. Lord, I see in Your Word that You hate pride, and I don't want to associate myself with anything You hate. Father, teach me Your way so that I can walk in the wisdom of Your Word. Lord, I thank You for giving me the wisdom and knowledge of Your Word so that I will be wise in all that I do to avoid the trap of the enemy. Father, I thank You that I will not be named among others as being prideful. Thank You, Lord, that I walk in a spirit of humility according to Your will and way for my life. In Jesus Name!

Thoughts and Prayers

His Name

His name is holy and above all names! He existed before the foundation of the earth because He spoke it into existence. His name is worthy of all the praise and worship that is due His Holy Name. If you had a thousand tongues, you couldn't give Him enough praise. His name is so powerful that our finite mind can't even reveal how great His name is. We can only stand in AWE of Him because He is all in all, the beginning and the end! God is eternal and the creator of everything! There is none like Him, and there will never ever be one like Him on earth or in heaven. God reigns forever in His infinite Spirit, power, and might. God redeemed us back to Himself through the Blood of Jesus Christ!

Scripture References

1 In the beginning God created the heavens and the earth. (Genesis 1:1)

6 For unto us a Child is born, Unto us a Son is given; and the government will be upon His shoulder. And His name will be called Wonderful, Counselor, Mighty God, Everlasting Father, Prince of Peace. (Israel 9:6)

18 Where is another God like you, who pardons the guilt of the remnant, overlooking the sins of his special people? You will not stay angry

with your people forever, because you delight in showing unfailing love. (Micah 7:18 NLT)

13 And suddenly there was with the angel a multitude of the heavenly host praising God and saying: 14 "Glory to God in the highest, And on earth peace, goodwill toward men!" (Luke 2:13–14)

16 For God so loved the world that He gave His only begotten Son, that whoever believes in Him should not perish but have everlasting life. (John 3:16)

23 But the hour is coming, and now is, when the true worshipers will worship the Father in spirit and truth; for the Father is seeking such to worship Him. 24 God is Spirit, and those who worship Him must worship in spirit and truth. (John 4:23–24)

Prayer

Father, thank You for being the great I Am, and there is none like You in all the earth. God, Your name is above all names, and there is no other name so great and powerful. Father, thank You for the love You demonstrated toward me when You sent Your only begotten Son, Jesus Christ, to die on the cross for my sins. Thank You, God, for redeeming me back unto Yourself making my eternal home in heaven with You. Glory to God in the highest. You are holy and worthy to be praised. Father, I worship You in Spirit and in truth, hallelujah, and I praise Your righteous and Holy Name! Father, if I had a thousand tongues, I couldn't speak of all the marvelous names that represent You! God, Your love never ends! Father, this is my prayer in Jesus Holy Name!

Thoughts and Prayers

Vengeance

Vengeance is similar to revenge, meaning a retaliation or a payback for something you feel you have been wronged. When you are exploiting with vengeance in your heart, you are opening the door for sickness (illnesses and diseases) in many types of form in your life. Satan will run rapid in your mind creating a battlefield filled with evil thoughts that will eventually be acted out if you don't get a grip and release the situation to the Lord. Vengeance is in the hands of Almighty God, and He can deal with it a lot better than we can. If you ever get in a situation where you want to take revenge, don't follow that spirit of evil because it can lead you to self-destruction.

Scripture References

1 Lord God, to whom vengeance belongs—O God, to whom vengeance belongs, shine forth! (Psalm 94:1)

17 I will execute great vengeance on them with furious rebukes; and they shall know that I am the Lord, when I lay My vengeance upon them. (Ezekiel 25:17)

15 And he said, "Listen, all you of Judah and you inhabitants of Jerusalem, and you, King Jehoshaphat! Thus says the Lord to you: 'Do not be afraid nor dismayed because of this great mul-

titude, for the battle is not yours, but God's.'" (2 Chronicles 20:15)

19 Beloved, do not avenge yourselves, but rather give place to wrath; for it is written, "Vengeance is Mine, I will repay," says the Lord. (Romans 12:19)

30 For we know Him who said, "Vengeance is Mine, I will repay," says the Lord. And again, "The Lord will judge His people." (Hebrews 10:30)

36 Therefore thus says the Lord: "Behold, I will plead your case and take vengeance for you." (Jeremiah 51:36)

2 God is jealous, and the Lord avenges; The Lord avenges and is furious. The Lord will take vengeance on His adversaries, and He reserves wrath for His enemies. (Nahum 1:2)

Prayer

Father, O merciful and mighty God of the universe, thank You for being my avenger. Lord, I ask You to forgive me for thinking I could take matters into my own hands. Thank You for the love You constantly demonstrate toward me even in taking revenge on my enemies when they come up against me. Lord, I thank You that I don't have to fight my battles. You say in Your Word that the battles are not mine; they belong to You when my adversaries come against me. God, I give You every situation concerning__________________ and surrender it/them into Your hands. In Jesus Name!

Thoughts and Prayers

Waiting

When you are waiting in a posture that seems so long and you feel like your patience is running thin, you are in the right position to call upon the One who can help you with life challenges and complex situations in your weakness. God is the source that can help you by strengthening and comforting you as you wait for a resolution to any problem or situation or life challenges that come your way. This is the time for you to seek God's help by praying to Him in Jesus Christ's Name and searching the Scriptures for knowledge pertaining to your situation for comfort, guidance, and direction. He has provided everything in the BIBLE (basic instruction before leaving earth) that you need for your life journey. Cling to God's Word with your faith; trust and believe God's Word as your final authority.

Scripture References

5 Trust in the Lord with all your heart, and lean not on your own understanding; 6 In all your ways acknowledge Him, and He shall direct your paths. (Proverbs 3:5–6)

5 May the Lord lead your hearts into a full understanding and expression of the love of God and the patient endurance that comes from Christ. (2 Thessalonians 3:5)

Prayer

Father, the great I Am, there is none like You. God, I thank You for being all-knowing and all-seeing in my life. Father, I thank You for leaving me guidance and direction for my life in Your Word. I thank You for strengthening and comforting me in my weaknesses as I wait on You, Lord! God, I don't lean to my own understanding and strength. I trust You, God. Thank You, Lord, for covering me with Your Spirit as I wait patiently on You for the resolution to this problem______________ or situation ______________ that is too complicated for me to handle on my own. God, I plead the Blood of Jesus in this area of my life today, and I am thanking You in advance for total and favorable results! In Jesus Christ Holy Name! Amen and Amen!

Thoughts and Prayers

Teens

If you are a teenager and are wondering where you fit in with other teens or peers, don't be the one that feels you have to fit into someone else's world to be accepted. As a teen, you are heading into a young adult with a lot of things going through your mind. Don't let one moment of pleasure or an irresponsible decision dictate your lifelong future. The decision that you make now will sometimes set a tone for your future or throw a curve ball to derail the pathway that has been established for you by God. The wrong decision can cause your pathway to take many detours before reaching your destiny that God has set for you. You can be the one that leads a productive life and make a difference in society to impact others to be ambitious and achieve great success. God created you with a plan and a purpose to bring glory and honor to Him. If you are having issues with your identity, have a conversation with your parents, a Christian leader, or seek out a trustworthy mentor to help compel you to your destiny that God has for you. Always remember you are great and fearfully and wonderfully created by God, and He will protect you.

Scripture References

13 For You formed my inward parts; You covered me in my other's womb. 14 I will praise You, for I am fearfully *and* **wonderfully** made; Marvelous are Your works, and *that* **my soul knows very well.** (Psalm 139:13–14)

10 The thief does not come except to steal, and to kill, and to destroy. I have come that they may have life, and that they may have it more abundantly. (John 10:10)

14 Because he has set his love upon Me, therefore I will deliver him; I will set him on high, because he has known My name. 15 He shall call upon Me, and I will answer him; I will be with him in trouble; I will deliver him and honor him. 16 With long life I will satisfy him, and show him My salvation. (Psalm 91:14–16)

11 For I know the thoughts that I think toward you, says the Lord, thoughts of peace and not of evil, to give you a future and a hope. (Jeremiah 29:11)

Prayer

Father, thank You that You are the creator and the protector of my life, and I don't have to follow anyone or participate in anything that will hinder the future and destiny You have set for me. Thank You, Lord, for strengthening me to know my identity and showering me with Your love. Thank You, Lord, for leading and guiding me when the enemy tries to lead me astray. Lord, I thank You for giving me parents with great intentions who are always directing me in the right path. Lord, I thank You for always putting someone in my path with great intention because You created me with a plan and purpose in mind. Father, help me to always choose to follow You and the plan You have for my life. In Jesus Name!

Thoughts and Prayers

Poor and Rich in Spirit

Poor in the spirit is not talking about your material possessions; it is talking about your state of spirituality with God. You have reached your lowest of the low by allowing sin to dominate you to the point where you have given the enemy control over your life. However, don't you forget that as long as you have breath in your body, you are able to call upon King Jesus with a repentant heart. Jesus will restore you back to righteousness and in the right fellowship with God when you allow Him to be first in your life. When you submit to God in humility through Jesus Christ and recognize the grace of God, then this is when you become rich in the spirit!

Scripture References

3 Blessed [spiritually prosperous, happy, to be admired] are the poor in spirit [those devoid of spiritual arrogance, those who regard themselves as insignificant], for theirs is the kingdom of heaven [both now and forever]. (Matthew 5:3 AMP)

9 For you are recognizing [more clearly] the grace of our Lord Jesus Christ [His astonishing kindness, His generosity, His gracious favor], that though He was rich, yet for your sake He became poor, so that by His poverty you might become rich [abundantly blessed]. (2 Corinthians 8:9 AMP)

Prayer

Father, thank You for being so gracious to me. I honor You in the Name of Jesus Holy Name. I praise You, God, and humble myself to You right now before Your throne room of grace asking You to forgive me for all my sins. Lord, I thank You for not leaving me lost and hopeless at the lowest point of my life. Father, I glorify Your righteous and Holy Name. Lord, if I had a thousand tongues, I couldn't give You enough praise for bringing me out of the hazardous lifestyle that was a danger to myself and others around me. God, I surrender all of me to You and ask that You would sanctify every part of me and make me fit for Your use. In Jesus Christ Matchless and Holy Name!

Thoughts and Prayers

Humility

Humility is feeling you are on even level with others and not above anyone else. You are not presenting yourself as prideful and puffed up with arrogancy. You are allowing the grace of God to rest upon you with a spirit of peace. You always treat others with the love of God and are quick to forgive. Always ask God for wisdom and discernment to live among others to avoid the cunning and craftiness of satan.

Scripture References

33 The fear of the Lord is the instruction of wisdom, And before honor is humility. (Proverbs 15:33)

12 Before destruction the heart of a man is haughty, And before honor is humility. (Proverbs 18:12)

4 By humility and the fear of the Lord are riches and honor and life. (Proverbs 22:4)

2 To speak evil of no one, to be peaceable, gentle, showing all humility to all men. (Titus 3:2)

12 Therefore, as the elect of God, holy and beloved, put on tender mercies, kindness, humility, meekness, longsuffering. (Colossians 3:12)

4 And in Your majesty ride prosperously because of truth, humility, and righteousness; And Your right hand shall teach You awesome things. (Psalm 45:4)

18 Let no one cheat you of your reward, taking delight in false humility and worship of angels, intruding into those things which he has not seen, vainly puffed up by his fleshly mind. (Colossians 2:18)

Prayer

Father, You are a great and mighty God, holy in all Your ways. I thank You, God, that You are a loving God who delights in the well-being of my life. Thank You for wrapping me with Your Spirit of grace allowing me to walk in humility. Lord, I thank You that I will not walk in a spirit of pride or arrogance. Father, I will allow Your Word to penetrate my heart so I will forgive quickly, live peacefully, and love others with the love of the Lord. Father, thank You for giving me the wisdom and power through the Holy Spirit to discern the trap of the enemy who comes with destruction for my life. God, thank You for granting me with Your blessings and benefits as a result of my humility. In Jesus Holy Name!

Thoughts and Prayers

Never Too Late

Never too late to change your lifestyle or go after your dreams in life when you commit to God and realize you can't do it on your own without God. When God created you as His masterpiece, He had a purpose in mind. If you have lost your way or don't know where to begin, I want to challenge you to start with your Creator for answers. God's loving arms are always open and waiting for you to return to Him. You may say I don't know where to begin; start by seeking God for forgiveness for not surrendering to Him for guidance and directions for your life. Create an environment for communication with God via your lifestyle through prayer, study the Word of God, build a relationship with God, keep your priorities and focus God-centered. Seek godly counsel from your spiritual leaders or parents or from someone you can receive wise counsel from. Live a humble lifestyle to represent God in all that you do. God can take your old life and conform it to His perfection.

Scripture References

33 The fear of the Lord is the instruction of wisdom, And before honor is humility. (Proverbs 15:33)

17 Therefore, if anyone is in Christ, he is a new creation; old things have passed away; behold, all things have become new. 18 Now all things are of God, who has reconciled us to Himself through

Jesus Christ, and has given us the ministry of reconciliation, 19 that is, that God was in Christ reconciling the world to Himself, not imputing their trespasses to them, and has committed to us the word of reconciliation. (2 Corinthians 5:17–19)

7 But what things were gain to me, these I have counted loss for Christ. 8 Yet indeed I also count all things loss for the excellence of the knowledge of Christ Jesus my Lord, for whom I have suffered the loss of all things, and count them as rubbish, that I may gain Christ 9 and be found in Him, not having my own righteousness, which is from the law, but that which is through faith in Christ, the righteousness which is from God by faith; 10 that I may know Him and the power of His resurrection, and the fellowship of His sufferings, being conformed to His death, 11 if, by any means, I may attain to the resurrection from the dead. (Philippians 3:7–11)

Prayer

Father, You are a great and mighty God, holy in all Your ways. I thank You, God, that You are an on-time God, and I thank You for never giving up on me even when I had given up on myself. Lord, thank You for giving me another chance and affording me the opportunity to realize in You all things are a new beginning. Father God, if I had a thousand tongues, I couldn't give You enough praise and adoration for You are worthy of all the praise and worship. Lord, You are giving me a new start in life. Father, only because of Your grace and mercy that I have a new mindset on life. Thank You for helping me to know through Christ by faith that I am redeemed by the Blood of Jesus! All things have become new, and in this new life, I can accomplish things I couldn't have accomplished without You being the head of my life. Thank You, Father! In Jesus Holy Name!\

Thoughts and Prayers

Church Hurt

What is church hurt? Well, it is not an excuse to not go to church. This is another old trick satan uses on saints to keep them from being delivered from emotional feelings/hurt and disappointments. Normally, the hurt is caused by someone in leadership or another saint. The enemy is telling you to stay home and not to go to church because you will be hurt again; this is a lie from the pit of hell. The Holy Spirit is beckoning you to come according to the Scriptures. You need to realize when you don't go to church, you are disobeying God's Word, and your emotional feelings are not a pass for you not to go to church. In fact, you need to run to the house of the Lord for your healing to avoid satisfying the human fleshly desire. The enemy wants to isolate you to destroy you. Saints never let someone else have that much power over you to keep you from the house of the Lord or hinder your healing from an offense sent from satan to destroy your life. No longer will you be held in bondage by an offense that hurt you. The flesh is always looking for a reason not to fellowship with the saints of God. Saints gather in the house of the Lord to share in their faith and to strengthen one another in the Lord.

Scripture References

24 Let us think of ways to motivate one another to acts of love and good works. 25 And let us not neglect our meeting together, as some people do, but encourage one another, especially

now that the day of His return is drawing near. (Hebrews 10:24–25 NLT)

10 The thief's purpose is to steal and kill and destroy. My purpose is to give them a rich and satisfying life. (John 10:10 NLT)

7 So humble yourselves before God. Resist the devil, and he will flee from you. 8 Come close to God, and God will come close to you. Wash your hands, you sinners; purify your hearts, for your loyalty is divided between God and the world. (James 4:7–8)

Prayer

Father, I pray and ask You to remove all the emotional hurt and feelings I am experiencing. I am thanking You in advance for strengthening me in my weakness to overcome struggles of situations that came to destroy me. Lord, I ask for strength to immediately release any hurt or disappointments to You in order for me to move forward in You. Help me to stay focused and to discern any attack of the enemy that come to destroy me. Father, thank You for drawing near to me as I draw near to You to strengthen my relationship with You. Thank You for a rich and satisfying life. In Jesus Name! Amen and Amen!

Thoughts and Prayers

Brief Testimony

On April 8, 2022, we were traveling to Alabama to check on Dricka, our niece, who was having a serious surgery dealing with her heart. Yes, we know God can hear our prayers from any place. We were just going for support since her mother, my sister, went on to glory almost two years ago.

We stopped at a LOVE gas station notice. I said LOVE. I had gone to the restroom, and when I came out, Greg, my husband, was talking to two men; you all know Elder Brewster doesn't meet any strangers, and HE loves to talk to people when he is in the right mood.

He said, "Hey honey, they are headed to Anniston, and I believe this may be Dricka's pastor (Word of Live Outreach Ministry)."

I said, "Well, let me ask her because I am waiting for her to answer the phone."

I asked Dricka what the name of her church was, and she said Word of Live Outreach Ministry, so I said Greg is talking to your pastor, and she started screaming in excitement! I was sitting in the truck at that time, and I never got out of the truck to meet him. He asked to speak to Dricka, so I handed my phone to Greg to give to him so he could speak to her. Nevertheless, after their conversation, we all departed the LOVE gas station.

About five minutes later, Greg's phone rang. It was the pastor, and he said I had to be obedient to God. He spoke to me and said, "You or your wife have been having pain in your hip." Greg looked like, *It isn't me this time.* I said, "It's me." At that point, I couldn't do anything *but* praise God because I had not told anybody but God!

God told him to tell me my pain will be gone by the time I reached *Alabama*! Also, God said, "Because you are an intercessor, the enemy has been coming against you." We know the enemy doesn't stop, but we *know who holds the power*! He said, "God said you have been wrestling with a lot of stuff you are believing HIM for, and it will come to pass." You all know God has not forgotten about us, and *I got my praise on* in that truck!!

I shared that to say God has not forgotten about you. He will use who He will to display His splendor and His handiwork, and He will do it how He pleases and when He wants to do it! But you got to be in position to be used, and this man was in position to deliver God's message to me, and I believed and received it. God manifested Himself to us in other ways at the church service that Sunday too, but I won't go into that.

Remember that you were created and fashioned by God's own hands!

> I praise You, for I am fearfully and wonderfully made; Marvelous are Your works, And that my soul knows very well! (Psalm 139:14)

About the Author

Wanda Brewster is a born-again believer believing the death, burial, and resurrection of Jesus Christ. She has firsthand knowledge of God's mercy and grace toward her. She loves to praise and worship God for His unfailing LOVE. God's Word is what she clings to for her daily living.

She has been married to Gregory Brewster Sr. for forty-three years. They have two adult children, Wendy Brewster-Murphy and Gregory Brewster Jr. She is currently serving as an Elder at New Beginnings Christian Church under the leadership of Pastor Ronnie Moore and First Lady Anita Moore. She is serving as one of the five ministers on the When I Rise I Worship (WIRIW) Ministry team under the leading of Minister Tammy Holloway.

Wanda is a graduate of the Sonship School of the Firstborn of Christian House of Prayer in Killeen, Texas. Wanda retired from the federal government with over thirty-two years of civilian service in June 2022.